A FIERCE
LION

OM JACKSON

Published in 2013 by Wayland
Copyright © 2013 Wayland

Wayland
338 Euston Road
London NW1 3BH

Wayland Australia
Level 17/207 Kent Street
Sydney NSW 2000

Editor: Julia Adams
Designer: Paul Cherrill
Picture researcher: Tom Jackson

Jackson, Tom.
  A fierce lion. -- (Animal instincts)
  1. Lion--Behavior--Juvenile literature.
  2. Lion--Life cycles--Juvenile literature.
  I. Title II. Series
  599.7'57-dc22

ISBN 978 0 7502 7856 0

The author and publisher would like to thank
the following agencies for allowing these pictures
to be reproduced:
All images and graphic elements: Shutterstock, apart
from: p. 8 (inset): Paul Souders/Corbis; p. 11 (all insets):
iStock; p. 12 (inset): STR/Reuters/Corbis; pp. 12/13:
Martin Harvey/Alamy; p. 1 and p. 14: Paul Souders/
Corbis; p. 15 (bottom inset): Dreamstime; p. 16: Ross
Warner/Alamy; p. 17 (top): Malcolm Schuyl/FLPA; p.
16 (bottom): David T. Grewcock/FLPA; p. 19 (top inset):
Dreamstime; p. 21 (skull): Dave King/Getty Images;
p. 22 (inset): Photos.com; p. 24: Mike Hill/Alamy; p.
25 (inset): Ace Stock Limited/Alamy; pp. 26/27: Steve
Bloom Images/Alamy; p. 28: AFP/Getty Images;
p. 29 (main image): Jon Hrusa/epa/Corbis.

Should there be any inadvertent omission,
please apply to the publisher for rectification.

Printed in China

10 9 8 7 6 5 4 3 2 1

Wayland is a division of Hachette Children's Books,
an Hachette UK company.
www.hachette.co.uk

CONTENTS

Mighty lions

Are you scared of lions? You probably should be. Attacks are very rare – lions don't usually hunt for people – but these big cats are one of the world's top **predators**.

The lion is the biggest cat living in **Africa**. It is also the noisiest, with its loud roars. Only lions and other "big cats" can roar. Smaller ones, like house cats, do not have the right voice box. They can only snarl and purr.

Fangs can rip through meat.

Padded paws mean lions can creep up on prey.

LION FACT FILE

Height:
male: 1.2 m; female: 1.1 m

Length:
male: 2.4 m; female: 1.8 m

Weight:
male: 240 kg; female: 160 kg

Average human:
height: 1.7 m; weight: 70 kg

Today most of the world's lions live in the south and east of Africa. They hunt on wide open grasslands, called **savannahs**. Lions were once found across **Asia**, but today, just a few hundred Asian lions survive in India.

Male has a thick mane to make him look big and strong.

No other cats have a tail tassel.

Eyes see in colour to help them spot their prey.

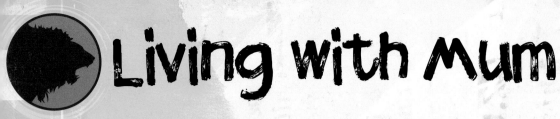

Living with Mum

A lioness gives birth to between one and four cubs. She finds a quiet place for her cubs to be born safely, out of sight of the other lions.

After we are born we sleep a lot and wait for Mum to feed us. Mum goes hunting from time to time. But she does not bring any food back for us. We only drink milk.

Lion cubs cannot see when they are born. Their eyes do not open until they are 11 days old. Hyenas, eagles and snakes often try to attack cubs when they are still blind.

A cub has marks on its fur. This means it can blend in better with the tall patchy grass.

Mum keeps us hidden when we are very young. She carries us to a clean and fresh den every few days, so predators can't sniff us out.

Mums lift their cubs by the skin on the back of their neck while they can't walk. It doesn't hurt them.

When we can walk, we go everywhere with Mum. We follow her tail tassel through the grass.

WOW!
A lion cub weighs 1.5 kg when it is born – that is about half the size of a human baby.

A cub can walk when it is 15 days old.

Joining the gang

Lions are the only cats that live in a family group, called a **pride**. When the cubs are two months old, their mum brings them to the pride for the first time.

Lion cubs purr when they are having fun.

There are lots of other cubs in the pride that are the same age as us. They all want to play! We pretend to be strong hunters, creeping through the grass. Sometimes we have big play fights, too.

I am never alone. The whole pride hunts, plays and rests together. We even clean our friends by licking their fur. Mum always makes sure I am clean.

I only met my dad after we joined the pride. He is huge! He doesn't play much. Now that I'm a bit older he has started getting really grumpy with me.

As male cubs grow up, the leader of the pride starts seeing them as a threat.

A lion's rough tongue combs out dirt and bugs.

IN THE KNOW

There are about 30 lions in a pride. Only one or two of those are adult males. They are very protective, so they won't let other males come close to the pride.

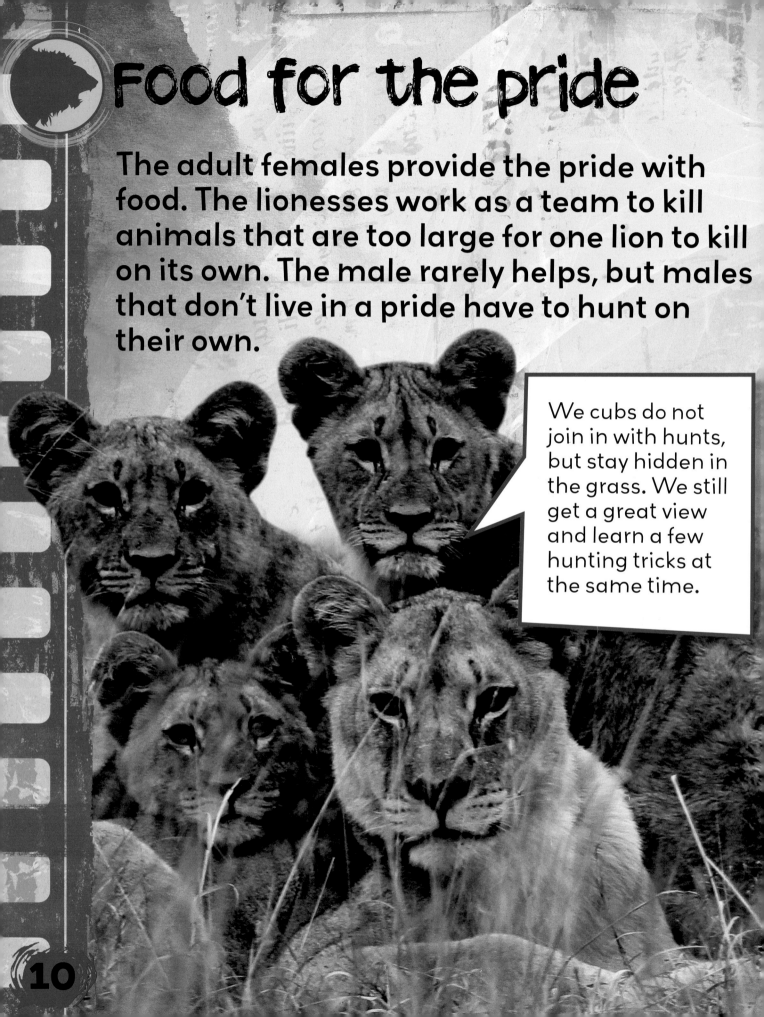

Food for the pride

The adult females provide the pride with food. The lionesses work as a team to kill animals that are too large for one lion to kill on its own. The male rarely helps, but males that don't live in a pride have to hunt on their own.

We cubs do not join in with hunts, but stay hidden in the grass. We still get a great view and learn a few hunting tricks at the same time.

Cubs eat their first meat at about three months old. They carry on drinking milk for a few more months. They can get milk from any lioness in the pride, not just their mother.

Lionesses take turns to look after the cubs while the other lionesses hunt.

The lionesses make sure the buffalo herd can see them.

But one lioness sneaks off to the other side of the herd...

Two lionesses start chasing a lone buffalo, driving it towards the hidden lioness.

The buffalo is trapped! The lionesses take turns to attack.

11

Meet the Neighbours

A lion pride has a **territory** – a home area just for them. The male defends it against lions from other prides. But there are plenty of other animals that pass through, whether the lions like it or not.

Almost every day, people pass through our territory. They are not hunting or grazing, but just come to watch us. They smell a bit funny, but the pride just ignore them.

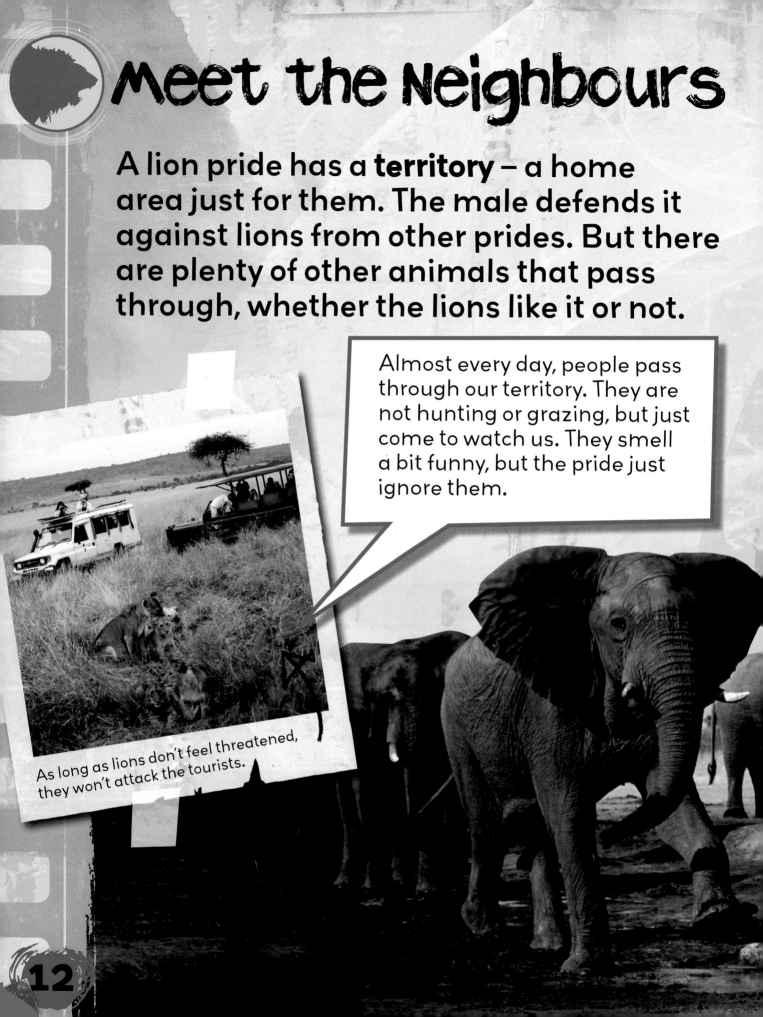

As long as lions don't feel threatened, they won't attack the tourists.

This large bird snatches lion cubs from their dens.

Martial eagle

A bite from a black mamba can kill a lion in just a few minutes.

Black mamba

NEIGHBOURHOOD WATCH

Spotted hyena

A hyena's bite is strong enough to crack the bones of a lion cub.

Crocodile

A Nile crocodile can kill a lion when it crosses a river.

Lions need to drink every day, but they will have to wait their turn this time.

Our pride is the fiercest of all. When we come to a waterhole, all the other animals leave. We can take as long as we want... until the elephants come. They are much bigger and stronger than us!

Forced out

When a male lion reaches about two years old, he will be forced to leave the pride by his father. This is before he grows strong enough to take over!

A big family makes life a lot easier. It is tough living away from the pride. Luckily my brother teamed up with me at first, which was a big help when we searched for food.

WOW!

An adult male lion is 80 kg heavier than a lioness and about three times as heavy as a man!

The mane begins to grow at the age of two. It will make the lion look even bigger and stronger.

I am growing quite strong, but not strong enough to fight the tough older males I meet. I have to keep my claws sharp by scratching them against trees and rocks, just in case I get attacked.

Claw marks and squirts of **urine** on trees signal that a new lion is in the area.

Claw action

Like all cats, lions keep their claws tucked into their paws, so they stay sharp. When the lion needs its claws, muscles flick each one into action.

When the lion's toes are relaxed, its claws are tucked in.

When it attacks, the lion stretches its toes, and the claws slide out.

sensors on

The growing lion is getting stronger every day. He uses his powerful senses to find food and tell his friends from his enemies.

When I crinkle up my face and take a deep breath, I can almost taste the air. I can smell other lions in the area and tell if they are a male or female. I can even tell if they are about to have cubs!

A lion's ears can turn to hear where a sound is coming from.

Lions can pick up smells with the roof of their mouth.

Lions eyes sometimes look like they are glowing in the dark.

> I do not go to sleep when the sun sets. I can see very well in the dark. Most animals have no idea I am here. But I need to watch out for other lions. If I can see them, they can see me.

Shining eyes

A lion's eye reflects light. This is because lions have a special layer in their eyes. Reflecting the light helps them see better in the dark. When the light is reflected, it looks like the eyes are glowing. All cats have this special layer in their eyes – even domestic cats.

Hunting alone

When a male lion hunts alone, most of his attacks fail. He can go for days without food, but if he doesn't get enough to eat he may never grow strong enough to become a pride leader.

It is hard for me to catch prey on my own. I hide in long grass and wait for something to come close enough to catch. I am always on the lookout for food.

Lions can recognise each other by the pattern of spots on the snout.

The lion pounces on the wilderbeest. His hook-shaped claws dig into its back.

The wilderbeest cannot escape the lion's grip and is pulled to the ground.

One bite to the wilderbeest's neck crushes the throat and kills it.

Now the lion has to stand guard over his prey, so hyenas don't steal any of it.

WOW!

A lion's mouth is big enough for a person's head to fit in!

Dinner time

A lion always sits down for its meals. It eats most of its prey, except the stomach, brain and bones.

I sometimes eat the leftovers from another hunter's kill, but fresh meat is much tastier! I always start by biting into the soft belly and eating what's inside. Then I move to the fleshy bottom and work my way to the head.

Lions use their fangs to grip flesh and rip off chunks of it.

The lion's rough tongue is great for licking scraps of meat off bones.

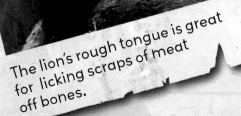

Lions cannot eat a whole wildebeest in one go. They need to have a rest before they can finish eating.

Lion skull and teeth

A lion's head is built for biting. The back half of the skull is covered in a huge muscle that pulls the jaw closed with great force. If the jaw gets injured, the lion cannot bite properly and the animal soon starves to death.

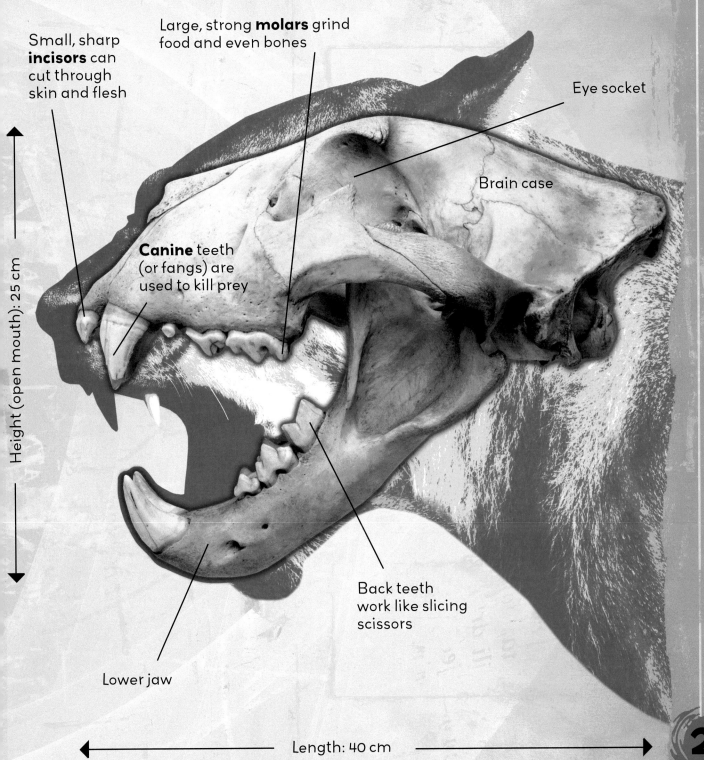

Small, sharp **incisors** can cut through skin and flesh

Large, strong **molars** grind food and even bones

Eye socket

Brain case

Canine teeth (or fangs) are used to kill prey

Height (open mouth): 25 cm

Back teeth work like slicing scissors

Lower jaw

Length: 40 cm

Taking a rest

The lion has eaten a lot and eaten it fast. A big male can gobble up 30 kg of food (the weight of a 10-year-old child) in about an hour. All that meat needs time to **digest**.

Back when I was in the pride, we cubs had to fight to get some food. But now that I'm on my own I can eat in peace – just like Dad used to. Right now I am so full, I cannot walk properly.

The skin on a lion's belly is folded so it can stretch to fit a stomach full of food.

Ready to fight

At about four or five years old, a male lion is ready to be pride leader. He can claim a territory and attract females from neighbouring prides to join him. Or he can fight and beat another chief lion.

After a few years on my own in the wild, I feel strong and ready to take on anything. I let other lions know this by roaring very loudly during the night.

A dark, thick mane is a sign that this male is very strong.

IN THE KNOW

Lions roar most at night when the air is still, so all the other lions in the area can hear them. You can hear a lion roaring 8 km away!

I have found a lioness from the local pride. Perhaps she saw the claw marks I had left in the area and wanted to set up home with me. She smells very nice...

Lions can smell when lionesses are ready to mate.

Before I can mate with the lioness, I have to fight the pride leader to take his place. I have to win the fight and chase him away.

A lion's mane protects from bites and scratches in a fight.

25

King of the pride

When a young lion wins his fight, the old leader moves away. The young lion becomes head of the pride. This means he has to protect the pride from danger, such as other lions.

Now that I am pride leader, I want to have my own cubs. But the lionesses are still busy taking care of the cubs from the old leader. I will have to kill them first.

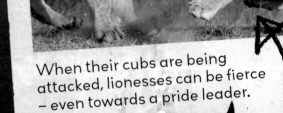

When their cubs are being attacked, lionesses can be fierce – even towards a pride leader.

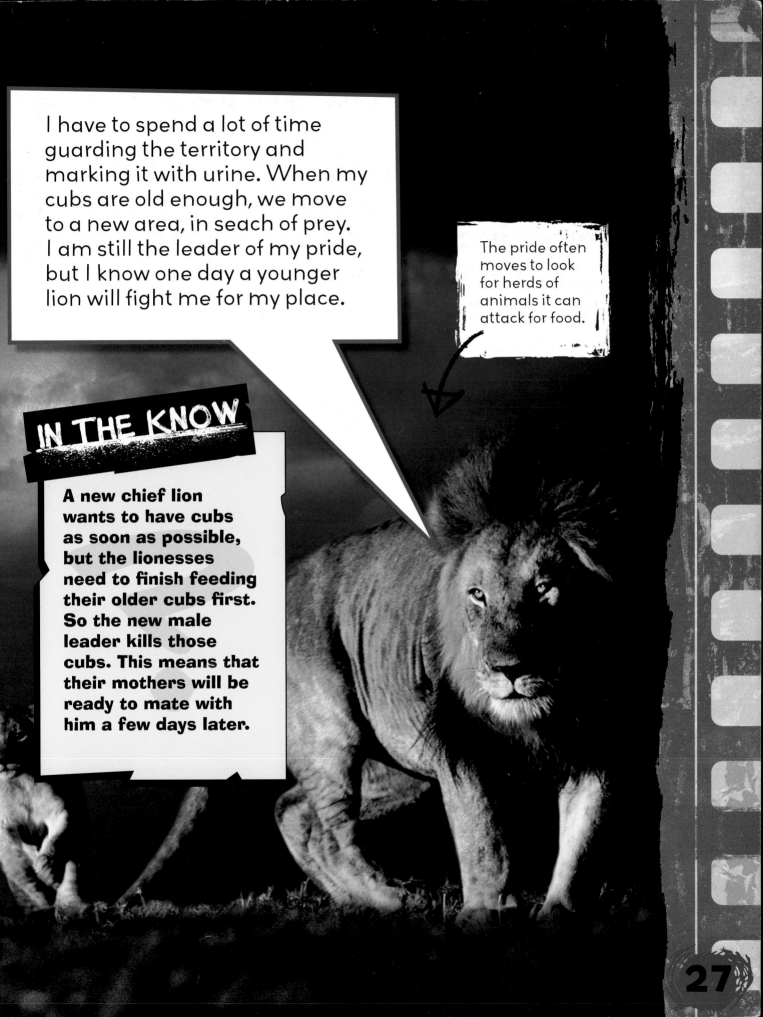

I have to spend a lot of time guarding the territory and marking it with urine. When my cubs are old enough, we move to a new area, in seach of prey. I am still the leader of my pride, but I know one day a younger lion will fight me for my place.

The pride often moves to look for herds of animals it can attack for food.

IN THE KNOW

A new chief lion wants to have cubs as soon as possible, but the lionesses need to finish feeding their older cubs first. So the new male leader kills those cubs. This means that their mothers will be ready to mate with him a few days later.

Saving lions

Africa's lions need to be protected because their numbers are going down. People who help protect animals are called **conservationists.** They work to make sure that lions will not die out.

The biggest threat to lions are humans. If a lion comes into a village, local people may shoot it, worried that it may attack them. Farmers also shoot lions to stop them killing their cattle. A lion cannot tell the difference between a farm animal and a wild one.

A farmer with a cow that has been killed by a lion.

Conservationists protect lions by moving them away from farms and villages. They first shoot each lion with a dart filled with sleeping drugs. The sleeping lion is put in a cage and moved to a safe area.

The sleeping drugs in the darts work after less than five minutes and send the lion to sleep for about two hours.

The best place to keep lions safe is in nature reserves. These are huge areas of land where farming is not allowed and very few people live. So the lions can live wild.

A fence stops lions from straying into dangerous areas.

QUIZ

1) Lions are like house cats. They spend most of their time alone. True or false?

2) Bones, legs, liver, eyeballs: Which one of these things do lions NOT eat?

3) Why do a lion's eyes appear to glow in the dark?

4) Can all types of cats roar?

5) Why are lion cubs born with marks?

6) Who does all the hunting for the pride?

7) How old are male lions when they start to grow a mane?

GLOSSARY

Africa A large continent, or area of land, that is in a warm part of the world. Africa includes countries like Egypt, Kenya and Nigeria

Asia The biggest continent on Earth which stretches half way around the world. Asia includes countries like India, China and Japan.

canine One of four long pointed fangs at the corners of the mouth. Lions use their canines to break the neck of their prey.

conservationist Someone who looks after endangered animals.

digest To break up food into its simple ingredients that can be taken in by the body and used to power the body.

incisor A small front tooth, used for cutting and nibbling; lions have eight incisors – the same number as a human.

molars The flat teeth at the back of the mouth that grind up food.

predator An animal that hunts for other animals and then kills them for food. Lions are one of the world's biggest predators.

pride A lion family with one or two males, several females and all their cubs.

savannah A dry grassland with only a few trees; lions live mostly on the savannahs of eastern and southern Africa.

territory The area controlled by a pride. Lion territories are huge – they are big enough to fit a large city inside.

urine Liquid waste produced by the body. Urine is also sometimes called wee. Lions and other animals use urine to leave smelly signals for each other and mark their territory.

Index